How Much Is a Little Girl Worth?

Rachael Denhollander

illustrated by Morgan Huff

Tyndale House Publishers, Inc.
Carol Stream, Illinois

Visit Tyndale's website for kids at tyndale.com/kids.

Visit the author's website at rachaeldenhollander.com.

TYNDALE is a registered trademark of Tyndale House Ministries. The Tyndale Kids logo is a trademark of Tyndale House Ministries.

How Much Is a Little Girl Worth?

Designed by Jacqueline L. Nuñez

Edited by Sarah Rubio

Published in association with the literary agency of United Talent Agency, LLC, 888 Seventh Avenue, 7th Floor, New York, New York 10106, USA.

For manufacturing information regarding this product, please call 1-855-277-9400.

For information about special discounts for bulk purchases, please contact Tyndale House Publishers at csresponse@tyndale.com, or call 1-855-277-9400.

Library of Congress Cataloging-in-Publication Data
Names: Denhollander, Rachael, author.
Title: How much is a little girl worth? / Rachael Denhollander.
Description: Carol Stream, Illinois : Tyndale House Publishers, Inc., 2019.
Identifiers: LCCN 2019011054 | ISBN 9781496441683 (hc)
Subjects: LCSH: Girls--Religious life--Juvenile literature. | Self-esteem
  in children--Religious aspects--Christianity--Juvenile literature.
Classification: LCC BV4551.3 .D465 2019 | DDC 248.8/2--dc23
LC record available at https://lccn.loc.gov/2019011054

Printed in China

27   26   25   24   23   22   21
9   8   7   6   5   4   3

Letter to Readers

I wrote this poem one night out of a deep need to answer a question I had been asking for the past two years: "How much is a little girl worth?" I wanted to answer it in a way that could communicate across generations. So many images flooded my mind as I wrote—my own three precious daughters, the little gymnasts I'd coached for years, and so many survivors of abuse, inside of whom I still saw the little girls they used to be. I saw all the times girls, small or grown, would ask, "Is this enough? Does this give me value?" as they pointed to their accomplishments or their bodies, their intellect or their friendships, trying to determine where their value came from and if they'd done enough to be worth something. I remembered the look of grief or fear in the eyes of little girls when they made a mistake, got a poor grade, heard hurtful words, or recounted trauma, mutely asking, "What am I worth now? Does this change who I am? Do you value me less?" And I saw all the times I had asked this question or felt this weight, sometimes not even understanding what I was asking in my own heart.

There are many voices competing to tell our daughters what they are worth, and most of them would teach our girls to define their value by something outside of themselves. By what they can do or what they wear or how they look or who their friends are. To live dependent on what others say about them and diminished by trauma they endure or mistakes they make. I believe one of the most important things we can do is stand against these voices that scream harmful messages into the ears of our little girls and instead whisper the truth to them over and over and over again.

Our daughters need to know that their worth is not derived from or dependent on external sources. It comes from how they were made. Our daughters need to know that their value is intrinsic to who they are, not based on what they can do or what others have done to them. Our daughters need to know whose voice to listen to and how to measure their value. This frees them from the social pressures that can threaten every facet of who they are; it frees them to heal when they have suffered; and it frees them to stand for what is right, no matter what anyone says.

Often, as I hold my little girls on my lap, I play a game we call "I love you more than . . ." We take turns thinking of the most amazing or beautiful things we've seen to describe how much my little girls are loved. "I love you more than every grain of sand . . . I love you more than the tallest mountain . . ." My hope is that as you read this book with your little girl, her heart will be filled with these truths. That she will be able to see the vast beauty and power of creation and know she is worth more than even these incredible things. That she will feel impressed upon her heart the reality that her value is not derived from what she accomplishes or what anyone else says. And that she will know she is of infinite worth because she is made in the image of her Redeemer. And I hope, in its childlike, simple way, that message will fill your heart too, because really, these are questions all of our hearts ask and truths all of us need.

With much love for every little girl, grown and small,
who needs to know how much she is worth,
Rachael

How much, how much
   are you worth, precious girl?
How much is a little girl worth?

More than the sun and the moon and the sky,
More than the shimmering sea.

All of the beautiful treasures of earth—
You are worth more than all that to me.

You're beautiful, worthy,
   and you should be loved
Because of all that you are.
Different from anything else in this world,
You are precious beyond all the stars.

You bear God's image—mind, body, and soul—
Lovingly made to be perfect and whole.

You are worth fighting for, raising my voice,
Worth every sacrifice, every hard choice.

Worth changing laws, worth all the fight,
Worth whatever it takes to do what is right.

11

Worth more than money or trophies or fame,
Worth more than power or protecting a name.

Worth speaking loudly to shout what is true,
Worth whispering softly how much I love you.

Worth running this race fast, hard, and strong,

Worth dancing slowly to your favorite song.

Worth fighting for justice, worth standing alone,
Worth whatever it takes for your worth to be shown.

How much, how much are you worth, precious girl?
How much is a little girl worth?

More than the sun and the moon and the sky,
More than the shimmering sea.
All of the beautiful treasures of earth—
You are worth more than all that to me.

Your value is found not in what you can do
Or the things you accomplish and win.
It is found in how you were made, precious girl—
Created and cherished by Him.

Your worth cannot fade; it will not go away;
It is not changed a bit by what happens today.

No one and nothing can make you worth less.

Just what is your value? You don't have to guess.

No one has power to change what God's done,
And He says you're worth everything, even His Son.

Worth all the pain, worth great sacrifice,
Worth leaving heaven, worth giving His life.

How much, how much are you worth, precious girl?
How much is a little girl worth?

Worth so much more than all my words could say—
No one and nothing can take that away.

To my precious daughters, Annaliese, Ellianna, and Elora—
may you always know your true value and rest in how deeply you are loved.

And to my own parents, whose sacrificial love and patient nurturing
first showed me how much a little girl is worth.

PAINTING BY JOAN MOXON

In loving memory of my Aunt Joan, whose childlike faith, gentle love, and delight in everything beautiful
and good taught me to find joy and hope in the world around me and my value in the Giver of Life.